Phytostabilization as a Remediation Alternative at Mining Sites

Technical Note 420

By:

Dennis Neuman
Reclamation Research Unit
Montana State University

and

Karl L. Ford
National Science and Technology Center
Bureau of Land Management

December 2006

Suggested citation:

Neuman, D. and K.L. Ford. 2006. Phytostabilization as a remediation alternative at mining sites.
  Technical Note 420. BLM/ST/ST-06/003+3720. Bureau of Land Management, Denver, CO. 48 pp.
  Online at *www.blm.gov/nstc/library/techno2.htm.*

Table of Contents

List of Figures

List of Tables

Abstract

In the last 10 years, the Bureau of Land Management (BLM) has reclaimed a number of abandoned mine land (AML) sites, often by removing mine, mill, and smelter wastes and taking them to a repository. This removal process involves excavating, hauling, placing, and capping tens of thousands of cubic yards of material, which can be quite costly.

BLM is seeking more cost-effective methods for reclaiming AML sites. Phytostabilization is a promising alternative for accomplishing the goals of a removal at a tenth of the cost. Phytostabilization is an in situ technology involving soil amendments and metals-tolerant plants to establish a ground cover that can reduce migration of metals to air, surface water, and ground water; reduce soil toxicity; and meet applicable, relevant, and appropriate requirements (ARARs). This technology has been found effective under certain conditions.

Through a 3-year applications of science (AOS) grant, BLM's National Science and Technology Center (NSTC) has worked with field offices and universities to pilot phytostabilization at two sites. This Technical Note summarizes the work done at the Keating tailings site near Butte, Montana, by Montana State University.

At the Keating tailings site, planting occurred in 2003. This year, which was the last year of the AOS grant, the test plots were in their third growing season. Canopy cover and aboveground biomass data have been collected, and samples have been analyzed for metal and arsenic concentrations. However, at least 1-2 years of additional monitoring of plant establishment and metals uptake sampling are required to verify the success of the technology and determine its feasibility for other AML sites on public lands.

1.0 Introduction

The public lands managed by the Bureau of Land Management (BLM) contain a large number of abandoned mine land (AML) sites, many of which are releasing contaminants, threatening human health and the environment, or violating environmental laws. BLM's Abandoned Mine Lands Inventory System (AMLIS) lists over 9,400 AML sites, most of which are from historic mining operations.

Active mine sites are being abandoned with greater frequency due to bankruptcy. These sites range from less than an acre to hundreds of acres. Abandoned sites differ from sites where active mines were closed in that they have no onsite presence and often no preclosure planning work was completed for them. Consequently, structures such as impoundments and dams have failed at these sites.

Research and demonstrations are needed to develop more cost-effective technologies appropriate for reclaiming BLM's AML sites. Phytostabilization is one such technology that shows promise (EPA 2000).

1.1 What is Phytostabilization?

Phytostabilization is the use of metals-tolerant plants to inhibit the mobility of metals, thus reducing the risk of further environmental degradation by leaching into ground water or by airborne spread (Salt et al. 1995). During phytostabilization, metals are chemically precipitated or sequestered by complexation and sorption mechanisms within the tailings or soils. Metal availability to plants is minimized, and metal leaching into ground water is reduced. Metals and arsenic that remain in soil solutions are demobilized via chemical reactions at plant root surfaces.

Plant species serve several purposes in phytostabilization. Plants harvest water in the rootzone and can transpire several hundred thousand gallons of water per acre during the growing season. This harvest has a significant impact on the volume of water (and metals and arsenic) that is able to move towards the ground water. Plants stabilize the landscape from erosion, greatly reducing surface water runoff and sediment available to receiving streams. Plants also reduce erosion caused by wind. Plant species are selected for phytostabilization based on the availability of their seeds or seedlings, their ability to thrive in the newly created rootzone, their lack of ability to translocate (or move) metals and arsenic from the roots into the aboveground biomass of the plant, and land use and management considerations.

There is a significant body of literature showing that phytostabilization is feasible under certain conditions. Phytostabilization has been found suitable for:

- Upland sites out of the flood plain
- Sites without shallow ground water
- Sites with low to moderate soil metals concentrations (as a point of departure depending on various factors: <1,500 ppm Cu+Pb+Zn+As+Cd+Hg)
- Repository sites, in place of an engineered cap
- As a partial component of a removal action involving several remedies, including repositories or capping

1.2 Application to Mining Sites

Environmental impacts at AML sites are highly variable, but many are characterized by high concentrations of toxic metals, cyanide, and acidity in mining waste that is released into surface water, ground water, and soils. The typical scenario is that tailings from historic mining operations reside in old, breached impoundments. Sometimes there are tolerant plant colonists established on tailings interspersed with bare tailings (called sickens), but frequently the tailings are devoid of vegetation. Bare tailings are available to release metals into the air as dust, into surface water by erosion and leaching, and into ground water by leaching. Bare tailings are not only toxic to plants, but also to fish and wildlife; thus, they represent a loss of habitat. Such sites may not comply with Federal and State environmental laws regulating air, water, and soil pollution and may be subject to enforcement.

Current cleanup methods usually involve removing and transporting contaminated materials to a disposal facility or isolating the mine wastes by capping them with clean fill. Both technologies are very expensive. For example, assume a repository action for a small 1-acre site with 10,000 cubic yards at a unit cost of $30-$100 per cubic yard. After removal, both the cleaned area and the repository need reclamation. The minimum cost under this scenario is $300,000-$1,000,000, not counting design, construction oversight, and other costs. Cleanup costs can range from $10,000 to $8 million per site.

Funding priority has been given to sites with tailings and rock dumps situated in stream channels and to sites that present significant human or ecological risk. Usually these sites are located on public lands used for recreation, grazing, wildlife, and water resources. Often these sites are remote from power and roads and may have restrictions because of designations of cultural resources, wilderness, or national conservation areas (e.g., San Pedro River).

Annual funding of $10 million is grossly inadequate to address the cleanup cost burden using current technologies. High-technology cleanup solutions employed by the Environmental Protection Agency (EPA) at Superfund sites are often not practical for remote, resource limited BLM sites. Cleanup costs for a single complex site can consume the entire annual budget. At present funding levels, it will take many years to clean up AML sites. It is very important, therefore, that lower cost cleanup alternatives be found for AML sites or their contaminants may end up polluting the environment for hundreds of years.

1.3 Phytostabilization Study

Through an Applications of Science (AOS) grant, the BLM and Montana State University's (MSU's) Reclamation Research Unit (RRU) have undertaken a study to investigate the use of phytostabilization to remediate the Keating tailings site near Butte, Montana. The objective of the study is to provide BLM managers and decisionmakers with site-specific information and data relating to the implementation, costs, and effectiveness of this technology so that it may be applied to other similar acid metalliferous mine tailing sites administered by the BLM. This work has been summarized in papers at the Environmental Protection Agency's (EPA's) International Phytotechnologies Conference in Atlanta in 2005, the National Association of Abandoned Mine Land Programs Annual Conference in Flagstaff in 2004 (Ford and Neuman 2004), and at the American Society of Mine Reclamation meeting in Breckenridge in June 2005 (Neuman et al. 2005).

AML sites have had the benefit of years of natural attenuation or restoration and, as such, are ideal laboratories to study the ecological effects of metals on plant communities and how to revegetate or phytostabilize tailings with plants. At present, literature on plant toxicity and plant tolerance is limited to agricultural crops and nonnative grasses. Little quantitative information is available for western range grasses, shrubs, and trees. This study employs public lands as a laboratory to examine the effects of metals toxicity on range plants.

Knowledge of plant toxicity to range plant communities typical of public lands is needed to determine whether, and under what conditions, soils and mining waste can be revegetated. Plant toxicity is also a function of acidity (often contributed by mine tailings) and other soil properties, such as organic matter and buffering capacity. Some mine waste is so toxic or acidic that it will require soil amendments to grow plants. This study addresses these issues as well as other questions concerning the extent to which plants will accumulate metals into their tissues and be available to the food chain and wildlife.

Knowing which native plants are tolerant to metals toxicity and how tailings may be amended to support plant species will lead to more cost-effective mine reclamation and restoration decisions. This crucial information may save scarce remediation and restoration dollars if amendments can be found to enable revegetation of mine tailings.

This study evaluates the ability of range plants to tolerate toxicity and adverse soil properties. In addition, it investigates the utility of inexpensive, locally available soil amendments in reclaiming old tailings and mine wastes, including waste manure from BLM wild horse and burro facilities, if available. Studying BLM sites with representative range plants and associated ecological conditions will lead to more cost-effective reclamations at AML sites, thus maximizing the benefit realized per dollar expended.

2.0 Study Design

The Keating tailings site is located in Broadwater County, Montana, on land administered by the BLM. These low pH (4 standard units or su) wastes resulting from historic gold and copper mining operations contain phytotoxic levels of several metals and are generally devoid of vegetation (Figure 1). With an estimated volume of 110,100 m³, these tailings represent an unacceptable risk to the environment and human health.

plants seeded into tailings that are not amended and plants seeded in an adjacent offsite, but non-impacted, area. This study design is intended to satisfy management and project objectives stated in the RRU statement of work (SOW) (RRU 2003) and in this Technical Note.

The research is being conducted in two phases. Phase I is the implementation of the experimental design at the Keating tailings. Phase II is the monitoring of vegetation responses and basic tailings chemistry as affected by phytostabilization. This Technical Note is a report of completed phase I activities and preliminary phase II findings.

Figure 1. Vegetation around the margins of the Keating tailings.

The study design involved constructing replicated experimental plots using soil amendments chosen to ameliorate the plant-inhibiting chemical characteristics of the tailings; seeding the experimental plots with appropriate native plants that can thrive in the newly created rootzone; monitoring vegetation response variables (specifically establishment, seedling density, cover, and aboveground biomass); and determining tailings pH, soil conductivity (SC), and soluble metal levels before and after treatment. The study compares the performance of vegetation grown in the amended or phytostabilized tailings to the performance of

2.1 Plot Setup and Soil/Tailings Sampling

Onsite and offsite study plots were surveyed and staked, with the perimeter corners of the test areas located using a Garmin IV Plus global positioning system (GPS) unit (Figures 2 and 3). Tailings and soil samples were collected from each of the plots using a Giddings soil probe. Three subsamples from each onsite plot were collected at 0- to 46-cm (0- to 18-in) increments and composited. In addition, three composite tailing samples were collected from 0 to 15 cm (0 to 6 in) and placed in new poly bags. Soil samples (0 to 15 cm) were also collected from the offsite plots using the Giddings soil probe. The samples were transported to the RRU at Montana State University, where they were dried and sieved to the < 2 mm fraction. These samples were characterized for several physicochemical parameters (Table 1).

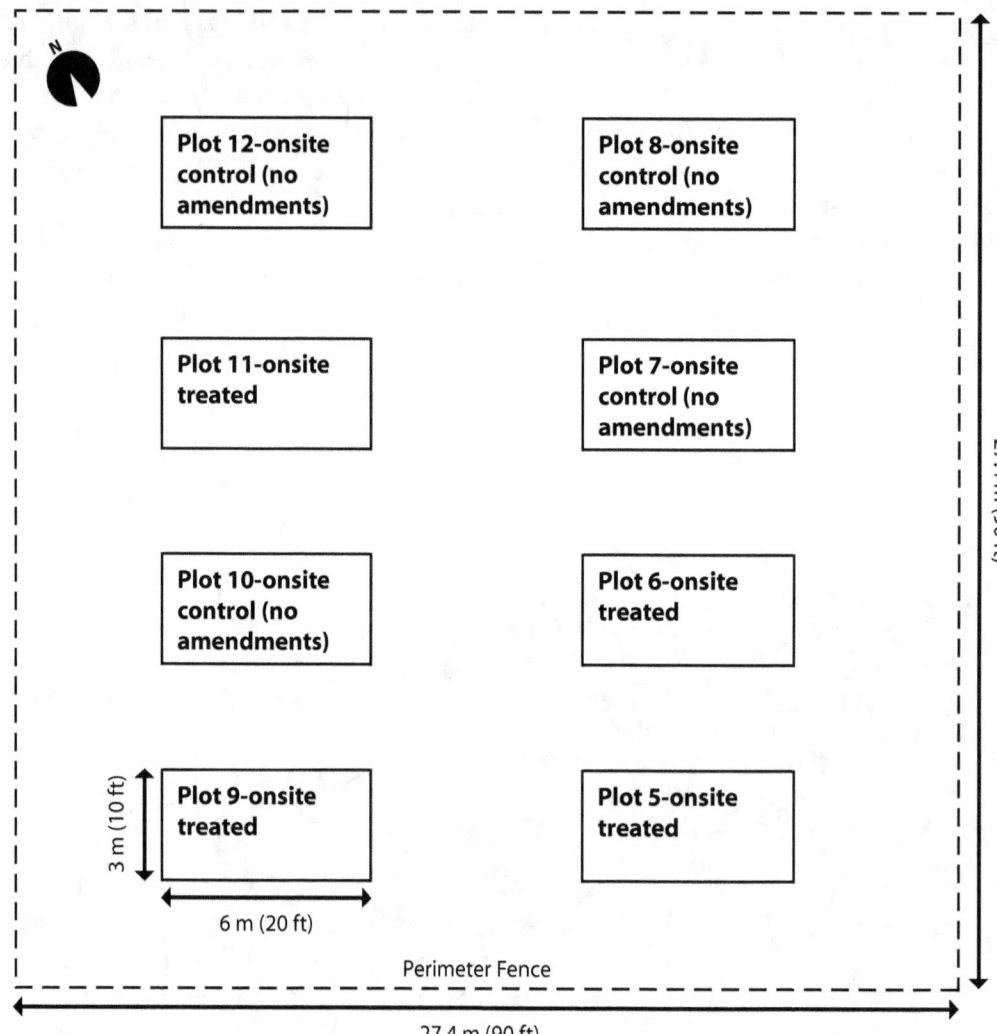

Figure 2. Schematic of onsite experimental plots.

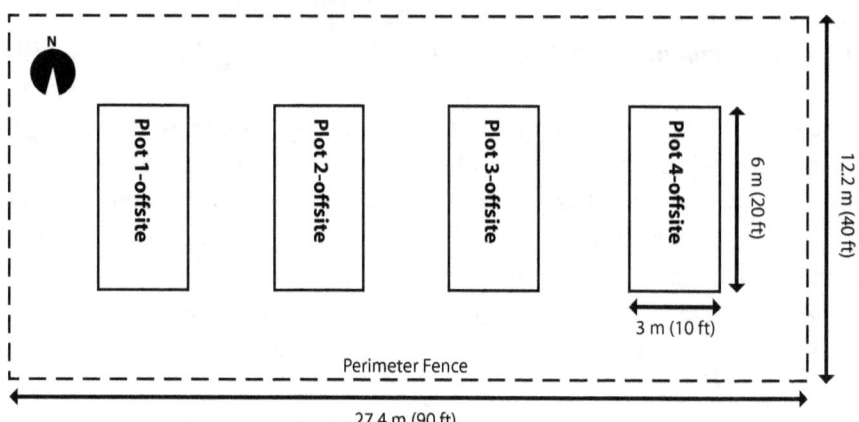

Figure 3. Schematic of offsite experimental plots.

Table 1. Soil and tailings analytical methods.

	CONSTITUENTS	METHOD
Soil Preparation	Separation for analysis of ≤ 2 mm fraction	ASTM D421-85 (ASTM 1997)
Percent Rock Fragments	Dry sieve analysis of rock fragments (> 2 mm) by volume and mass	ASTM D422-63[1] (ASTM 1997)
Particle Size, Soil Textural Class	Hydrometer method for soil texture, USDA classification	ASA Method 15-5 (ASA 1986)
Saturation Percent	Saturation percent by weight of water to soil	ASA Method 21-2.2.2 (ASA 1986)
Sodium Adsorption Ratio	Soil fraction	Method 3.2.19 (Sobek et al. 1978)
Electrical Conductivity	Saturated paste extract	USDA Handbook 60, Method 3a, 4b (U.S. Salinity Lab Staff 1969)
pH	Saturated paste extract	USDA Handbook 60, Method 3a, 21c (U.S. Salinity Lab Staff 1969)
Total As and Metals, Soluble As and Metals	As, Cd, Cu, Pb, Hg, Co, Cr, Fe, Mn, Ni, and Zn	Standard EPA CLP methods (www.epa.gov/super-fund/programs/clp) for soluble metals in saturated paste extracts. Total metals by BLM using x-ray fluorescence methods.
K	Fertilizer requirement	Method 13-3.5 (ASA 1982)
$NO_3.N$, $NH_4.N$	Fertilizer requirement	Method 4500 F, H (APHA 1989)
P	Fertilizer requirement	Bray -P, Method 24-5.1 (ASA 1982)
Total Organic Matter	Based on organic carbon	Method 29-3.5.2 (ASA 1982)

[1] Modifications to ASTM D422-63 include volumetric determination of the percent retained on the No. 10 sieve. The set of sieves specified in ASTM D422-63 reduced to only the No. 10 sieve and any larger mesh sieves necessary for optimum laboratory efficiency.

2.2 Analytical Results

Soil and tailing metal levels were analyzed by Ashe Analytics using an x-ray fluorescence (XRF) device (Table 2). The Niton XRF device has both cadmium and americium source materials. The samples were analyzed for arsenic (As), cadmium (Cd), copper (Cu), mercury (Hg), manganese (Mn), lead (Pb), and zinc (Zn). Water extractable metal levels were determined from saturated paste extracts by the Soil Testing Laboratory at Montana State University (Table 3). The extracts were filtered and acidified, then analyzed using an inductively coupled atomic emission spectrophotometer calibrated for the metals analyzed.

Total As values determined by Ashe Analytics ranged from 30.4 mg/kg for soils collected from the offsite study area to a maximum of 334 mg/kg on plot 11. Background As values ranged from 1.2 to 97 mg/kg for 490 soil samples in the Western U.S. (Munshower 1994). Adriano (1986) lists background As values in normal soils from 0.2 to 40 mg/kg. Water extractable arsenic levels ranged from 0.43 to 0.84 mg/kg. Munshower (1994) reports water extractable arsenic levels in normal soils at "presumably" less than 1 mg/kg. Arsenic is more toxic to animals than plants, but can be phytotoxic when plant tissue levels increase up to 20 mg/kg (Munshower 1994).

The maximum total Cd value from Ashe Analytics was 5.3 mg/kg for a composite sample collected from plot 10 on the tailings site. Water extractable Cd levels were up to 6.26 mg/kg in the plot 12 soil composite. Total background levels for Cd in soils is less than 3 mg/kg (Munshower 1994) with an average of 1.6 mg/kg for alluvial soils (Adriano 1986). Phytotoxicity responses to Cd have been noted in values as low as 0.5 mg/kg added to solution, with responses in tall fescue and alfalfa ranging from 95 to 30 mg/kg added to soil (Adriano 1986).

Table 2. Tailings and soil metal levels determined by Ashe Analytics using a laboratory-grade XRF. Samples collected on July 9, 2003.

Sample ID	Plot No. Depth	As (mg/kg)	Cd (mg/kg)	Cu (mg/kg)	Hg (mg/kg)	Mn (mg/kg)	Pb (mg/kg)	Zn (mg/kg)
1	Plot 1 (offsite) 0-6"	30.7	<4.2	43.8	<7.5	1140.0	30.4	105.0
2	Plot 2 (offsite) 0-6"	33.2	<4.2	42.3	<7.5	1090.0	31.1	110.0
3	Plot 3 (offsite) 0-6"	30.4	<4.2	50.7	<7.5	1080.0	30.3	114.0
4	Plot 4 (offsite) 0-6"	30.7	<4.2	46.0	<7.5	1140.0	26.8	101.0
5	Plot 5 (onsite treated) 0-18"	26.0	<4.2	281.0	<7.5	637.0	181.0	611.0
6	Plot 6 (onsite treated) 0-18"	279.0	<4.2	300.0	<7.5	1180.0	271.0	870.0
7	Plot 7 (onsite control) 0-18"	276.0	<4.2	329.0	<7.5	1130.0	258.0	924.0
8	Plot 8 (onsite control) 0-18"	274.0	4.5	327.0	<7.5	1570.0	256.0	1110.0
9	Plot 9 (onsite treated) 0-18"	312.0	4.4	414.0	<7.5	1360.0	323.0	1170.0
10	Plot 10 (onsite control) 0-18"	305.0	5.3	356.0	<7.5	1480.0	289.0	1170.0
11	Plot 11 (onsite treated) 0-18"	334.0	<4.2	358.0	<7.5	1380.0	273.0	1170.0
12	Plot 12 (onsite control) 0-18"	310.0	<4.2	341.0	<7.5	1340.0	233.0	1020.0
13	Plot 11 Duplicate	322.0	<4.2	344.0	<7.5	1420.0	287.0	1210.0
14	2710 NIST* Standard	621.0	21.8	2990.0	31.2	10000.0	5520.0	6940.0

* National Institute of Standards and Technology

Table 3. Water extractable metal (saturated paste extract) determined by inductively coupled plasma (ICP) at Montana State University Soil Testing Laboratory. Samples collected on July 9, 2003.

Sample ID	Plot No. Depth	As (mg/kg)	Cd (mg/kg)	Co (mg/kg)	Cr (mg/kg)	Cu (mg/kg)	Fe (mg/kg)	Mg (mg/kg)	Mn (mg/kg)	Ni (mg/kg)	Pb (mg/kg)	Zn (mg/kg)
1	Plot 1 (offsite) 0-6"	0.66	<0.03	<0.07	<0.08	0.07	<0.17	93.69	0.21	<0.07	<0.28	<0.03
2	Plot 2 (offsite) 0-6"	0.68	<0.04	<0.07	<0.08	0.08	<0.17	76.00	0.24	<0.07	<0.28	<0.03
3	Plot 3 (offsite) 0-6"	0.77	<0.05	<0.07	<0.08	0.09	<0.17	90.00	0.23	<0.07	<0.28	<0.03
4	Plot 4 (offsite) 0-6"	0.43	<0.06	<0.07	<0.08	0.06	<0.17	52.00	0.23	<0.07	<0.28	<0.03
5	Plot 5 (onsite treated) 0-18"	0.47	0.68	0.84	0.52	2.40	<0.17	2358.00	183.00	1.83	<0.28	51.60
6	Plot 6 (onsite treated) 0-18"	0.62	2.64	1.29	0.62	33.80	0.39	2637.00	325.00	2.97	0.56	135.00
7	Plot 7 (onsite control) 0-18"	0.61	3.45	1.56	0.74	28.90	0.54	3114.00	363.00	3.79	<0.28	202.00
8	Plot 8 (onsite control) 0-18"	0.61	4.91	1.84	0.75	10.60	0.61	2864.00	665.00	5.39	0.61	269.00
9	Plot 9 (onsite treated) 0-18"	0.79	6.18	4.03	0.86	62.40	0.93	2732.00	960.00	8.99	0.93	398.00
10	Plot 10 (onsite control) 0-18"	0.72	5.51	2.36	0.86	31.20	0.86	3079.00	871.00	7.73	0.79	338.00
11	Plot 11 (onsite treated) 0-18"	0.74	6.19	3.46	0.74	47.80	1.03	2580.00	727.00	7.37	0.88	390.00
12	Plot 12 (onsite control) 0-18"	0.84	6.26	3.87	0.91	51.50	1.05	3374.00	1003.00	9.63	0.91	433.00
13	Plot 11 Duplicate	0.73	5.53	2.98	0.95	33.50	1.02	2690.00	694.00	7.27	0.87	385.00

Copper values ranged from 42.3 mg/kg in the offsite control soils to 358 mg/kg in tailings from plot 11 compared to typical background soil values of 3 to 50 mg/kg (Munshower 1994). Phytotoxic effects have been noted in soils with a pH greater than 6.5 for total soil Cu values in the range of 1062-1636 mg/kg (USEPA and MDEQ 1998). Water extractable values ranged from 0.06 to 62.4 mg/kg. Using the water extractable fraction of Cu in the soil as a conservative estimate of the labile portion available to plants, yields have been reduced in plants such as spring wheat, sugar beets, and maize above 2 mg/kg Cu in solution (Adriano 1986).

Manganese levels in the tailings and soil ranged from 637 to 1570 mg/kg for total values. Water extractable levels, which are presumably labile to plants, ranged from 0.21 mg/kg for the offsite soils to a maximum of 1003 mg/kg for plot 12 on the tailings site. Manganese toxicity to plants generally occurs when soil pH levels are less than 5.5 (Adriano 1986). Water extractable levels of Mn at 2.5 mg/kg in soils with pH of <5.5 have been found to be toxic to plants (Munshower 1994). The low pH values in the tailings (< 5.6) and high Mn values are well within this phytotoxic range (Table 4).

Zinc levels determined by Ashe Analytics were elevated (611-1210 mg/kg) in the tailings material compared to the offsite control soils (101-114 mg/kg). Water extractable values were <0.03 in the offsite soils and ranged from 51.6 to 433 mg/kg in the tailings material. Zinc is a required plant nutrient, but phytotoxic response has been shown with DTPA extractable values from 50 to 150 mg/kg (Munshower 1994). Adriano (1986) reported phytotoxic effects in corn in acid soils from extractable Zn values of 450 to 1400 mg/kg.

Soil pH, texture, percent organic matter, and other physicochemical analytical results vary widely between the offsite soils and the tailings material (Table 4). Tailings pH values are all below the desired range of 6.5 to 8.5 su, while the offsite control soils are all near 8.5 su. The tailings material textures are all classified as silt loam or silt, while the offsite soils range from sandy clay loam to clay loam. A comparison with cover soil criteria for the Anaconda area (U.S. EPA and MDEQ 1998) shows that many of the tailings samples exceed the upper limit for conductivity of 4.0 dS/m and have very little organic matter All of the sodium absorption ratio (SAR) values are less than 4, indicating that the tailings and offsite soils are within the "normal" soil range (Sobek et al. 2000). Rock content was less than 1 percent for all samples.

Table 4. Cations and other physicochemical results from Montana State University Soil Testing Laboratory. Samples collected on July 9, 2003

Sample ID	Plot No. Depth	Na (mg/L)	Ca (mg/L)	pH	SAR	Conduct. (dS/m)	H$_2$O (%) sat. paste	Sand (%)	Silt (%)	Clay (%)	USDA Texture	Organic Matter (%)	NO$_3$ as N (mg/kg)	Olson P (mg/kg)	K (mg/L)
1	Plot 1 (offsite) 0-6"	39	79	8.5	1.0	0.71	34.7	50	24	26	sandy clay loam	2.19	0.8	12.9	342
2	Plot 2 (offsite) 0-6"	13	98	8.4	0.3	0.66	40.2	54	24	22	sandy clay loam	2.60	0.9	13.9	356
3	Plot 3 (offsite) 0-6"	113	33	8.5	3.8	0.74	45.2	42	22	36	clay loam	1.90	0.8	11.8	276
4	Plot 4 (offsite) 0-6"	109	30	8.5	3.9	0.70	28.8	56	24	20	sandy clay loam	1.56	0.5	10.6	228
5	Plot 5 (onsite treated) 0-18"	55	506	5.6	0.4	3.81	52.4	18	76	6	silt loam	0.23	2.9	40.1	172
6	Plot 6 (onsite treated) 0-18"	77	497	4.2	0.6	4.18	56.1	16	78	6	silt loam	0.17	6.9	38.8	134
7	Plot 7 (onsite control) 0-18"	85	496	4.1	0.7	4.24	67.7	12	84	4	silt	0.22	5.8	35.1	168
8	Plot 8 (onsite control) 0-18"	164	497	4.5	1.3	4.30	68.2	8	88	4	silt	0.19	8.9	36.0	150
9	Plot 9 (onsite treated) 0-18"	102	538	4.2	0.8	4.26	71.9	4	90	6	silt	0.09	71.1	33.3	124
10	Plot 10 (onsite control) 0-18"	115	516	4.3	0.9	4.36	71.6	7	88	5	silt	0.19	38.5	28.3	146
11	Plot 11 (onsite treated) 0-18"	90	508	4.2	0.8	4.03	73.7	5	90	5	silt	0.19	7.4	38.4	136
12	Plot 12 (onsite control) 0-18"	94	582	4.2	0.7	4.16	70.3	5	90	5	silt	0.11	10.4	36.0	136
13	Plot 11 Duplicate	89	508	4.3	0.7	3.95	72.7	3	92	5	silt	0.08	6.7	36.6	140

3.0 Research Results

In the first growing season, 2004, response variables, including emergence and establishment, density, and canopy cover, were evaluated. Concentrations of metals in vegetation were evaluated in terms of plant sufficiency or excess and in terms of maximum allowable dietary levels for cattle. Changes in soil rootzone pH, conductivity, and soluble metal concentrations before and after treatment were also determined. Results from these data were presented by Neuman et al. (2005).

In July 2005, the vegetation growing on the 12 experimental plots at the Keating tailings pond was evaluated. Canopy cover by species within each plot was determined using the Daubenmire's cover class method (Daubenmire 1959). Samples of aboveground plant material were collected by clipping, drying, and weighing. Rooting patterns were evaluated by developing excavation pits with selected plots. Digital images were collected and field notes were written. Samples of dried vegetation were submitted to BLM for determination of metal (cadmium, copper, lead, mercury, and zinc) and arsenic concentrations.

3.1 General Comments Regarding the Site in July 2005

Heavy spring rains in 2005 stimulated excellent plant growth on the treated tailings plots (refer to Figures A-1 and A-2 in Appendix A). Slender wheatgrass (*Elymus trachycaulus*) and western wheatgrass (*Pascopyrum smithii*) were approximately 48 inches tall (Figure A-3). All seeded species, except American vetch (*Vicia americana*), were found on all of the treated plots. The vetch was noticeably absent and occurred as an incidental species in one treated plot. Several nonseeded plant species established in the treated plots. The onsite untreated tailings plots (controls) had sparse vegetation (Figure A-4) limited to three of the seeded species: western wheatgrass, slender wheatgrass, and big bluegrass (*Poa ampla*). Evidence of rodent activity, most likely from meadow voles (*Microtus pennsylvanicus*) or white-footed deer mice (*Peromyscus* sp.), was present in the treated tailings plots but not on the control plots. The offsite plots on native soils supported very good plant growth (Figure A-5). Many species were present that were not in the seed mix, but the plots were dominated by slender wheatgrass. Many other native species were also present. Yellow sweetclover (*Melilotus officinalis*) was prevalent on the surrounding hillsides (Figure A-1), but absent from all experimental plots.

3.2 Canopy Cover

Five 20- x 50-cm frames were placed along a diagonal transect on each plot. Cover class for each individual species within the frame was recorded. Canopy cover of perennial grasses and forbs determined in 2004, 2005, and 2006 are exhibited in Table 5 and Appendix B. Kruskal-Wallis one-way analysis of variance by ranks revealed that the median cover value for perennial grasses growing on the control tailings plots in 2004 was significantly less than the cover of these species growing on the offsite native soil plots and the treated tailings plots (Table 5).

Table 5. Comparison of perennial grass and forb canopy cover on the experimental plots.

Plots	Median Perennial Grass Canopy Coverage (%)	Mean Forb Canopy Coverage (%)	Mean Shrub and Subshrub Canopy Coverage (%)
2004 Data			
Treated Tailings	62.5 a[1]	6.25 a	ND
Control Tailings	15.0 b	1.50 b	ND
Offsite Soils	62.5 a	2.25 b	ND
2005 Data			
Treated Tailings	65.0 a	3.0 a	0.0
Control Tailings	10.1 b	0.0	0.0
Offsite Soils	39.0 a	2.6 a	5.0
2006 Data			
Treated Tailings	66.6 a	3.1 a	0.0
Control Tailings	11.3 b	0.0	0.0
Offsite Soils	52.8 a	4.3 a	3.9

[1] Values followed by same letter in columns are not significantly different ($P < 0.05$).

Mean forb canopy cover measured in 2004 was significantly less for the offsite native soils compared to the forb cover on the treated tailings plots.

Analysis of variance indicated that the percent cover of perennial grasses growing on the treated tailings in 2005 is significantly ($P < 0.05$) greater than percent canopy cover of perennial grasses growing on the control tailings. Canopy cover of vegetation on the treated tailings was not statistically distinct from perennial grasses growing on the offsite plots. The percents of canopy cover of forbs growing on the treated tailings and the offsite plots were also statistically equivalent. This same statistical pattern of canopy cover was found in 2006.

3.3 Species List

A species list of all plants found within each of the 12 experimental plots was developed (Table 6). Species are distinguished by whether they were part of the seed mix or naturally established within the plot. The detailed vegetation cover data were used to designate major species with a mean cover of greater than 0.5 percent for the plot and those species that were present during the July survey but contributed little to the overall vegetation cover of the plot.

Table 6. Species occurring on each experimental plot of the Keating tailings project, 2005.

Scientific Name	Common Name	Seeded Species (Y/N)	Offsite Native Soils 1	2	3	4	Treated Tailings 5	6	9	11	Untreated Tailings 7	8	10	12
Achillea millefolium	Common yarrow	Y	M	X	M	M	M	M	M	M		X		X
Achnatherum hymenoides	Indian ricegrass	Y	M	M	M	M	X	X	X	M				X
Artemisia frigida	Prairie sagewort	Y	M	M	M	M		X	X	X				
Artemisia ludoviciana	Cudweed sagewort	Y	M	M		M	X	X	X	X				
Artemisia tridentata	Big sagebrush	N					X	X	X	X				
Astragalus spp.	Milkvetch	N				M								
Brassica nigra	Black mustard	N		X	X									
Chenopodium berlandieri	Pitseed goosefoot	N						X		X				
Chrysothamnus nauseosus	Rubber rabbitbrush	N							X					
Elymus trachycaulus	Slender wheatgrass	Y	M	M	M	M	M	M	M	M	M	M	M	M
Festuca L.	Fescue	N			M									
Gutierrezia sarothrae	Broom snakeweed	N	X	X	X	X		X						
Hesperostipa comata	Needle and thread	N	M	M	M	M		X	X					
Hordeum jubatum	Foxtail barley	N	X		X	X	X	X	X	X				
Hordeum L.	Barley	N	X	X	X	X								X
Lepidium densiflorum	Common pepperweed	N		X		M								
Nassella viridula	Green needlegrass	Y	M	M	M	M	X	M	M	M				
Opuntia polyacantha	Plains pricklypear	N	M			X								
Pascopyrum smithii	Western wheatgrass	Y	M	M	M	M	M	M	M	M	M	M	M	M
Plantago patagonica	Woolly plantain	N				X				X				
Poa ampla	Big bluegrass	Y	M	M		M	M	M	X		M	M	X	M
Poa spp.	Bluegrass	N						X	X	X		X	X	
Polygonum aviculare	Prostrate knotweed	N						X	X	X				
Polygonum lapathifolium	Curlytop knotweed	N						X	X	X				
Populus tremuloides	Quaking aspen	N					X				X	X	X	X
Potentilla L.	Cinquefoil	N												X
Sphaeralcea coccinea	Scarlet globemallow	N		M		X		X	X	X				
Tragopogon dubius	Yellow salsify	N			X			X	X					
Unknown	Ground lichen	N				X								
Verbena bracteata	Bigbract verbena	N								X				
Vicia americana	American vetch	Y		X										X
Number of Species			13	15	14	18	10	16	15	14	4	6	5	8

M = major species with > 0.5% cover, X = other species occurring in the plot.
Plots 1-4 are offsite native soils; plots 5, 6, 9, and 11 are onsite treated tailings; plots 7, 8, 10, 12 are onsite control.

3.4 Aboveground Biomass

A 25- x 25-cm frame was placed in the same location as the cover frame, and vegetation with each frame was clipped, segregated by plant species, and placed into separate labeled paper bags for transport to the RRU labs. The samples were oven dried (70° C) for 24 to 36 hours. The vegetation mass in each bag was weighed to the nearest 0.01 gram. Mean aboveground biomass of live vegetation in grams/m² is displayed in Figure 4. Analysis of variance indicated significant differences ($P < 0.05$) among the three mean values, with the treated tailings supporting the greatest aboveground plant biomass, followed by the offsite native range soils.

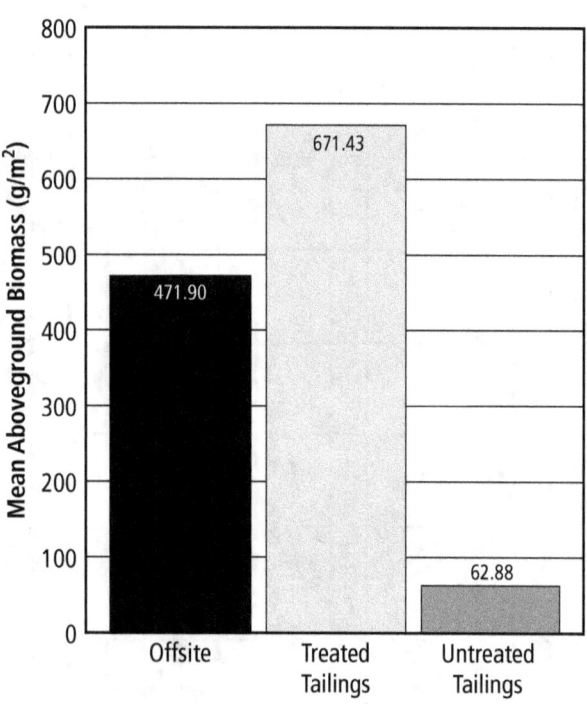

Figure 4. Mean aboveground biomass.

The untreated tailings did support some plant growth, but it was significantly less than the treated tailings and offsite native range soils. Two grasses, western wheatgrass and slender wheatgrass contributed most to the biomass on all plots and treatments (refer to Appendix C for biomass data for each species and plot).

3.5 Metal Levels in Vegetation

Vegetation samples collected for biomass determinations were submitted to BLM in Denver for determination of concentrations of selected elements, including arsenic, cadmium, lead, copper, zinc, and mercury. Mean levels of these elements in grass samples [western wheatgrass, slender wheatgrass, Indian ricegrass (*Achnatherum hymenoides*) and big bluegrass] collected from the experimental plots are provided in Figures 5 and 6. The complete data set of elemental levels in vegetation is provided in Appendix D.

Arsenic in Vegetation

Analysis of variance indicated that the mean arsenic level in grasses growing on the untreated tailings (2.60 mg/kg) was significantly greater than mean concentrations for grasses growing on treated tailings (1.09 mg/kg). Grasses growing on the native range soils revealed the least arsenic, with a mean of 0.36 mg/kg. For these statistical tests, any arsenic value reported at the detection limit was multiplied by 0.7, with the resulting value used to calculate mean concentrations. Based on a review of the scientific literature (Kabata-Pendias and Pendias 1992), normal or sufficient levels of arsenic in mature leaf tissue range from 1 to 1.7 mg/kg; excessive or toxic levels for plants range from 5 to 20 mg/kg. None of the individual grass samples collected from the experimental plots had arsenic levels in the excessive range. The maximum tolerable dietary level of arsenic for cattle and horses (NRC 1980) is 50 mg/kg. The arsenic concentrations in grasses growing on the Keating tailings do not pose a threat to grazing animals.

Cadmium in Vegetation

The mean concentration of cadmium in samples collected from the untreated tailings was 3.23 mg/kg, which was not statistically distinct from the mean cadmium concentration of grasses collected from the treated plots (0.70 mg/kg). A significantly lower mean concentration of cadmium was found in grasses growing on the native soils (0.04 mg/kg).

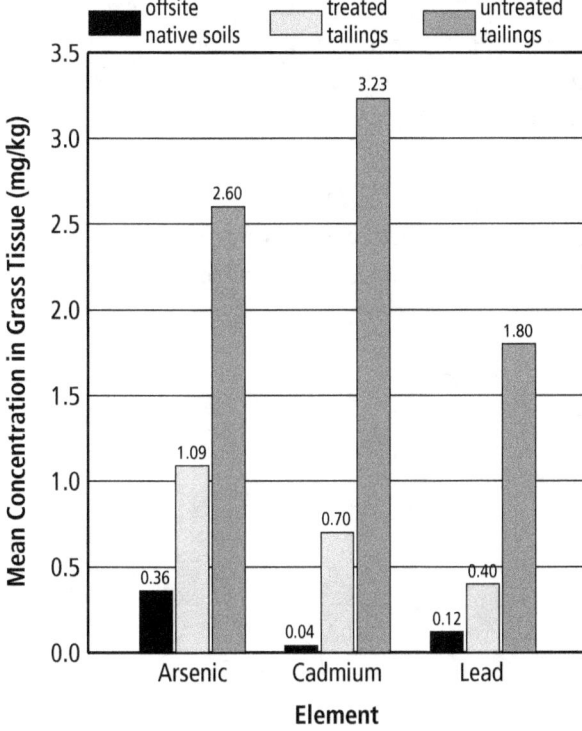

Figure 5. Mean concentrations of arsenic, cadmium, and lead in grass samples.

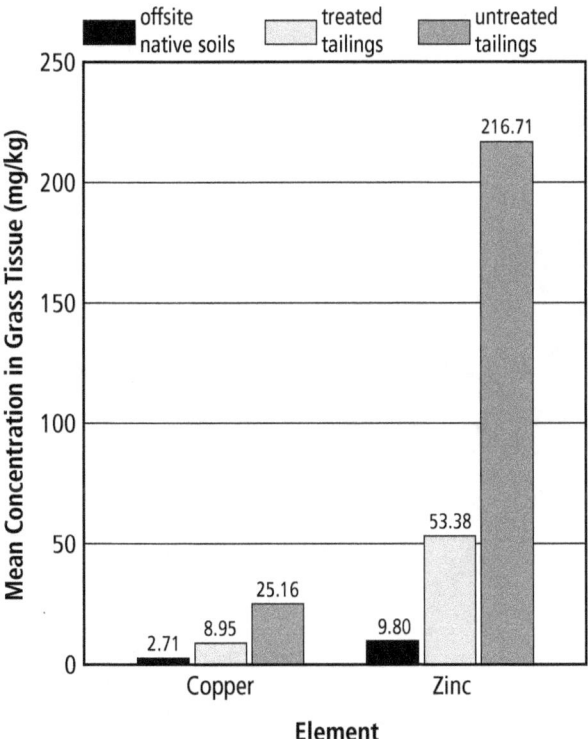

Figure 6. Mean concentrations of copper and zinc in grass samples.

The maximum tolerable dietary level of cadmium for cattle and horses is 0.50 mg/kg (NRC 1980). Of the eight individual grass samples from the treated tailings (refer to Appendix D), one sample of Indian ricegrass was found to have a cadmium concentration of 2.13 mg/kg, while the other samples had cadmium concentrations ranging from 0.21 to 0.80 mg/kg. The dietary level of cadmium for domesticated animals is based on human food residue considerations (NRC 1980) and the need to avoid increases of cadmium in the U.S. food supply. Higher residue levels (>0.50 mg/kg) for a short period of time would not be expected to be harmful to animal health or to human food use, particularly if the animals were slaughtered at a young age (NRC 1980).

Lead in Vegetation

Lead levels in vegetation samples were relatively low. Analysis of variance indicated that the mean concentration of lead in grasses growing on the untreated tailings (1.80 mg/kg) was significantly elevated compared to mean levels in grasses growing on the treated tailings (0.40 mg/kg) or native range soils (0.12 mg/kg). All concentrations were less than the maximum tolerable dietary level for cattle and horses of 30 mg/kg (NRC 1980). Normal concentrations of lead in mature leaf tissue range from 5 to 10 mg/kg (Kabata-Pendias and Pendias 1992). All lead levels were below this range (refer to Appendix D). The lead concentrations in grasses growing on the Keating tailings do not pose a threat to grazing animals.

Copper in Vegetation

Mean concentrations of copper in grass samples collected from the site were significantly different across the three treatments (Figure 6). The grasses growing in offsite native range soils had a mean copper level of 2.71 mg/kg. This level would be considered in the deficient range for this essential element. Mean levels of copper in grasses growing on treated and untreated tailings, 8.95 and 25.16 respectively, are statistically different (P < 0.05), but within the sufficient or normal range of 5 to 30 mg/kg provided by (Kabata-Pendias and Pendias 1992). The maximum tolerable dietary level of copper for cattle and horses is

100 mg/kg (NRC 1980). The copper concentrations in grasses growing on the Keating tailings do not pose a threat to grazing animals.

Zinc in Vegetation

Mean zinc concentrations were quite variable (Figure 6), and analysis of variance found that they were statistically distinct. The maximum dietary level of zinc for cattle and horses is 500 mg/kg

(NRC 1980); no sample concentration exceeded this value. The zinc concentrations in grasses growing on the Keating tailings do not pose a threat to grazing animals.

Mercury in Vegetation

All of the mercury values were < 0.1 mg/kg (refer to Appendix D). No interpretation of the data is necessary.

4.0 Future Directions

Phytostabilization takes advantage of soil amendments and metals- and acid-tolerant plants to revegetate sites. In so doing, metals are immobilized, for the most part, and are not available for migration or exposure. Proper selection of amendments is necessary to ensure growth; proper selection of plants is also necessary to ensure growth and to prevent bioaccumulation.

The Bridger USDA Natural Resources Conservation Service (NRCS) Plant Materials Center has collected and cultivated metals-tolerant plants from the Anaconda Superfund site and released varieties of basin wild rye, fuzzytongue penstemon, and common snowberry. The Center plans to release additional species for metals-contaminated sites, including slender wheatgrass, western wheatgrass, bluebunch wheatgrass, big bluegrass, silverleaf phacelia, woolly cinquefoil, Woods' rose, silver buffaloberry, western snowberry, and horizontal juniper. These native species, along with introduced species such as redtop and tufted hairgrass should be considered for BLM sites in the Rocky Mountain states. Future work should be performed to identify metals-tolerant species for other BLM states.

Recent field studies by MSU RRU suggest that there is an upper threshold on the total toxic metals concentration for which phytostabilization is effective. Soil amendments can help neutralize acidity and precipitate metals to a point, after which the technology may be ineffective. Work by RRU suggests this threshold can be estimated by the following regression equation (Jennings and Neuman 2006):

$$\text{Total Metals } [As+Cd+Cu+Pb+Zn] = 520 \times pH - 2300$$

For example, at a pH of 7.0, when the sum of metals is greater than 1,340 mg/kg, phytotoxic conditions are expected with increasing severity as the sum of metals increases above the threshold.

In other recent work, MSU RRU performed soil greenhouse toxicity studies to assess the phyto-toxicity of actual site soils with metal mixtures [As+Cd+Cu+Pb+Zn] to reclamation plants (Martin and Neuman 2006). Metals-tolerant plants such as slender wheatgrass, basin wildrye, and blue bunchgrass were evaluated. Mine waste "soils" were neutralized with lime and diluted with control soil into various doses. This work suggests that biomass is reduced by 50 percent for slender wheatgrass at about 3500 mg/kg, for basin wildrye at 2600 mg/kg, and for blue bunchgrass at 2800 mg/kg. The slope of the dose response curve suggests that 10 percent biomass reduction is found for these species at 700 mg/kg, 700 mg/kg, and 900 mg/kg total metals, respectively. However, soil is a complex medium and other soil factors such as texture and organic matter may affect phytotoxicity. Greenhouse studies such as these can help ensure the success of reclamation work, especially if other plant species are phytostabilization candidates.

For sites with more than about 1,300 mg/kg total metals as defined above, capping with topsoil or cover soil will be more effective than in situ phytostabilization.

References Cited

Adriano, D.C. 1986. Trace elements in the terrestrial environment. Springer-Verlag, New York. 533 pp.

ASA (American Society of Agronomy). 1986. Methods of soil analysis: Part 2-Chemical and microbiological methods. 2nd edition. Klute, A. (ed). American Society of Agronomy and Soil Science Society of America, Madison, WI.

ASA (American Society of Agronomy). 1982. Methods of soil analysis. Page et al. (ed). Agronomy Monograph No. 9. SMP Single Buffer Method, 12-3.4.4.4. Madison, WI. pp. 215-217.

APHA (American Public Health Association). 1989. Standard methods for the examination of water and wastewater. 17th edition. Clesceri, L.S., A.E. Greenberg and R.R. Trussell (eds). Washington, DC.

ASTM (American Society for Testing and Materials). 1997. Annual book of ASTM standards. Vol. 4.01 and 4.08. West Conshohocken, PA.

Daubenmire, R. 1959. A canopy-coverage method of vegetational analysis. Northwest Science 33:43-64.

Ford, K.L and D. Neuman, 2004. Phytostabilization of abandoned mine sites. Proceedings of the 26th Annual National Association of Abandoned Mine Land Program Conference, Flagstaff, AZ.

Jennings, S. and D. Neuman. 2006. Phytotoxic constraints to vegetation establishment at the Anaconda Smelter Superfund site. Billings Land Reclamation Symposium, Billings MT.

Kabata-Pendias, A. and H. Pendias. 1992. Trace elements in soils and plants. CRC Press, Boca Raton, FL. 365 pp.

Martin, T. and D. Neuman. 2006. Differential plant response to plants to varying levels of metals and arsenic to lime-amended contaminated soils. Billings Land Reclamation Symposium, Billings, MT.

Munshower, F.F. 1994. Practical handbook of disturbed land revegetation. CRC Press, Boca Raton, FL. 265 pp.

Neuman, D.R., G.S. Vandeberg, P.B. Blicker, J.D. Goering, S.R. Jennings, and K. Ford. 2005. Phytostabilization of acid metalliferous mine tailings at the Keating site in Montana. In: Proceedings of the 2005 National Meeting of the American Society of Mining and Reclamation, Breckenridge, CO. Published by ASMR, 3134 Montavesta Road, Lexington, KY 40502.

NRC (National Research Council). 1980. Mineral tolerance of domestic animals. National Academy of Sciences, Washington, DC. 577 pp.

RRU (Reclamation Research Unit). 2003. Revised work plan for phytostabilization studies at the Keating tailings site. Prepared by Reclamation Research Unit, Montana State University for Karl Ford, U.S. Department of the Interior, BLM, Denver, CO.

Salt, D.E. et al. 1995. Phytoremediation: A novel strategy for the removal of toxic metals from the environment using plants. Bio/Technol. 13: 468-474.

Sobek, A.A., J.G. Skousen, and S.E. Fisher, Jr. 2000. Chemical and physical properties of overburden and mine soils. In Barnhisel, R.I., R.G. Darmody, and W.L. Daniels (eds). Reclamation of drastically disturbed lands. Agronomy Monograph No. 41; ASA, CSSA, and SSA; Madison, WI.

Sobek, A.A., W.A. Schuller, J.R. Freeeman, and R.M. Smith. 1978. Field and laboratory methods applicable to overburdens and mine soils. EPA-600/2-78-054. U.S. Environmental Protection Agency Technology, Cincinnati, OH. 203 pp.

USEPA (U.S. Environmental Protection Agency) and MDEQ (Montana Department of Environmental Quality). 1998. Record of decision. Anaconda Regional Water, Waste and Soils Operable Unit. Helena, MT.

USEPA (U.S. Environmental Protection Agency). 2000. Introduction to phytoremediation. EPA/600/R-99/107. National Risk Management Laboratory. Cincinnati, OH.

U.S. Salinity Laboratory Staff. 1969. Diagnosis and improvement of saline and alkali soils. Agricultural Handbook No. 60. U.S. Department of Agriculture, Washington, DC. 160 pp.

Appendix A–Site Photos from July 2005

Figure A-1. An overview of experimental plots on Keating tailings, July 6, 2005. Note apparent difference between treated tailings and untreated tailings.

Figure A-2. The treated tailings plots.

Figure A-3. A treated plot with yarrow in flower along the plot edge and the stand dominated by the seeded wheatgrasses.

Figure A-4. Untreated (control) tailings plots.

Figure A-5. Offsite experimental plots on native soils.

Figure A-6. Treated tailings pit face and roots sprayed with Hellige pH indicator solution. The pH of the tailings is approximately 7 to 8.

Figure A-7. Untreated (control) tailings pit face and roots sprayed with Hellige pH indicator solution. The pH of the tailings is approximately 4.5.

Appendix B–Canopy Cover of Vegetation

Table B-1. Vegetation cover at Keating tailings, July 7, 2005.

PLOT 1 - Offsite Native Range Site

Life Form and Species	Frame 1 Class	Frame 1 Midpoint Percent	Frame 2 Class	Frame 2 Midpoint Percent	Frame 3 Class	Frame 3 Midpoint Percent	Frame 4 Class	Frame 4 Midpoint Percent	Frame 5 Class	Frame 5 Midpoint Percent	Mean Cover per Plot
Perennial Grasses											
Hesperostipa comata	1	2.5			1	2.5					1.0
Poa ampla	1	2.5	1	2.5					1	2.5	1.5
Pascopyrum smithii	1	2.5	2	15.0	1	2.5	1	2.5	1	2.5	5.0
Elymus trachycaulus	2	15.0	3	37.5	2	15.0	3	37.5	3	37.5	28.5
Nassella viridula							1	2.5			0.5
Achnatherum hymenoides									1	2.5	0.5
Total Perennial Grasses		22.5		55.0		20.0		42.5		45.0	37.0
Perennial Forbs											
Artemisia ludoviciana			1	2.5	1	2.5					1.0
Achillea millefolium			1	2.5							0.5
Total Perennial Forbs		0.0		5.0		2.5		0.0		0.0	1.5
Shrubs and Subshrubs											
Artemisia frigida	2	15.0	1	2.5	2	15.0	1	2.5			7.0
Opuntia polyacantha	1	2.5									0.5
Total Shrubs and Subshrubs		17.5		2.5		15.0		2.5		0.0	7.5
Sum of Species Cover		40.0		62.5		37.5		45.0		45.0	46.0
Total Live Vegetation Cover		40.0		62.5		37.5		45.0		45.0	46.0
Litter	1	2.5	2	15.0	2	15.0	2	15.0	2	15.0	12.5
Mulch	1	2.5	1	2.5	3	37.5	2	15.0	3	37.5	19.0
Bare ground	2	15.0	1	2.5	1	2.5	1	2.5	1	2.5	5.0
Total Ground Cover		45.0		80.0		90.0		75.0		97.5	77.5

Table B-2. Vegetation cover at Keating tailings, July 7, 2005.

PLOT 2 – Offsite Native Range Site

Life Form and Species	Frame 1 Class	Frame 1 Midpoint Percent	Frame 2 Class	Frame 2 Midpoint Percent	Frame 3 Class	Frame 3 Midpoint Percent	Frame 4 Class	Frame 4 Midpoint Percent	Frame 5 Class	Frame 5 Midpoint Percent	Mean Cover per Plot
Perennial Grasses											
Hesperostipa comata					1	2.5			1	2.5	1.0
Poa ampla					1	2.5			1	2.5	1.0
Pascopyrum smithii	1	2.5	1	2.5	1	2.5	1	2.5	1	2.5	2.5
Elymus trachycaulus	3	37.5	3	37.5	2	15.0	3	37.5	2	15.0	28.5
Nassella viridula			1	2.5							0.5
Achnatherum hymenoides			1	2.5	1	2.5			1	2.5	1.5
Total Perennial Grasses		40.0		45.0		25.0		40.0		25.0	35.0
Perennial Forbs											
Artemisia ludoviciana	1	2.5	2	15.0	1	2.5					4.0
Total Perennial Forbs		2.5		15.0		2.5		0.0		0.0	4.0
Shrubs and Subshrubs											
Artemisia frigida	1	2.5	2	15.0					2	15.0	6.5
Sphaeralcea coccinea							1	2.5			0.5
Total Shrubs and Subshrubs		2.5		15.0		0.0		2.5		15.0	7.0
Sum of Species Cover		45.0		75.0		27.5		42.5		40.0	46.0
Total Live Vegetation Cover		45.0		75.0		27.5		42.5		40.0	46.0
Litter	2	15.0	2	15.0	2	15.0	2	15.0	1	2.5	12.5
Mulch	2	15.0	2	15.0	2	15.0	3	37.5	2	15.0	19.5
Bare ground	1	2.5	1	2.5	0		0		2	15.0	4.0
Total Ground Cover		75.0		105.0		57.5		95.0		57.5	78.0

Table B-3. Vegetation cover at Keating tailings, July 7, 2005.

PLOT 3 – Offsite Native Range Site

Life Form and Species	Frame 1 Class	Frame 1 Midpoint Percent	Frame 2 Class	Frame 2 Midpoint Percent	Frame 3 Class	Frame 3 Midpoint Percent	Frame 4 Class	Frame 4 Midpoint Percent	Frame 5 Class	Frame 5 Midpoint Percent	Mean Cover per Plot
Perennial Grasses											
Hesperostipa comata	1	2.5	1	2.5							1.0
Pascopyrum smithii	1	2.5	1	2.5	2	15.0	1	2.5	1	2.5	5.0
Elymus trachycaulus	2	15.0	3	37.5	4	62.5	3	37.5	2	15.0	33.5
Nassella viridula	1	2.5									0.5
Achnatherum hymenoides			1	2.5							0.5
Festuca L.	1	2.5									0.5
Total Perennial Grasses		25.0		45.0		77.5		40.0		17.5	41.0
Annual Grasses											
Hordeum L.			1	2.5							0.5
Total Annual Grasses		0.0		2.5		0.0		0.0		0.0	0.5
Perennial Forbs											
Artemisia ludoviciana	1	2.5					1	2.5	1	2.5	1.5
Achillea millefolium							1	2.5			0.5
Total Perennial Forbs		2.5		0.0		0.0		5.0		2.5	2.0
Shrubs and Subshrubs											
Artemisia frigida	1	2.5							1	2.5	1.0
Total Shrubs and Subshrubs		2.5		0.0		0.0		0.0		2.5	1.0
Sum of Species Cover		30.0		47.5		77.5		45.0		22.5	44.5
Total Live Vegetation Cover		30.0		47.5		77.5		45.0		22.5	44.5
Litter	1	2.5	2	15.0	2	15.0	2	15.0	1	2.5	10.0
Mulch	1	2.5	2	15.0	2	15.0	2	15.0	2	15.0	12.5
Bare ground	3	37.5	1	2.5	0		1	2.5	3	37.5	16.0
Total Ground Cover		35.0		77.5		107.5		75.0		40.0	67.0

Table B-4. Vegetation cover at Keating tailings, July 7, 2005.

PLOT 4 – Offsite Native Range Site

Life Form and Species	Frame 1 Class	Midpoint Percent	Frame 2 Class	Midpoint Percent	Frame 3 Class	Midpoint Percent	Frame 4 Class	Midpoint Percent	Frame 5 Class	Midpoint Percent	Mean cover per plot
Perennial Grasses											
Hesperostipa comata	1	2.5			1	2.5					1.0
Poa ampla	1	2.5	2	15.0	1	2.5			1	2.5	4.5
Pascopyrum smithii	2	15.0	1	2.5	1	2.5	2	15.0	1	2.5	7.5
Elymus trachycaulus	3	37.5	2	15.0	3	37.5	3	37.5	2	15.0	28.5
Nassella viridula			1	2.5					1	2.5	1.0
Achnatherum hymenoides			1	2.5	1	2.5					1.0
Hordeum jubatum					1	2.5					0.5
Total Perennial Grasses		57.5		37.5		50.0		52.5		22.5	44.0
Perennial Forbs											
Artemisia ludoviciana			1	2.5	1	2.5	1	2.5			1.5
Achillea millefolium									1	2.5	0.5
Lepidium densiflorum	1	2.5									0.5
Astragalus spp.					1	2.5					0.5
Total Perennial Forbs		2.5		2.5		5.0		2.5		2.5	3.0
Shrubs and Subshrubs											
Artemisia frigida	1	2.5	1	2.5	1	2.5			2	15.0	4.5
Total Shrubs and Subshrubs		2.5		2.5		2.5		0.0		15.0	4.5
Sum of Species Cover		62.5		42.5		57.5		55.0		40.0	51.5
Total Live Vegetation Cover		62.5		42.5		57.5		55.0		40.0	51.5
Litter	2	15.0	2	15.0	2	15.0	2	15.0	2	15.0	15.0
Mulch	2	15.0	2	15.0	2	15.0	2	15.0	3	37.5	19.5
Bare ground	2	15.0	1	2.5	1	2.5	1	2.5	1	2.5	5.0
Total Ground Cover		92.5		72.5		87.5		85.0		92.5	86.0

Table B-5. Vegetation cover at Keating tailings, July 7, 2005.

PLOT 5 - Onsite Treated with Lime and Organic Matter

Life Form and Species	Frame 1		Frame 2		Frame 3		Frame 4		Frame 5		Mean Cover per plot
	Class	Midpoint Percent	Class	Midpoint Percent	Class	Midpoint Percent	Class	Midpoint Percent	Class	Midpoint Percent	
Perennial Grasses											
Poa ampla									1	2.5	0.5
Pascopyrum smithii	3	37.5	1	2.5	1	2.5	2	15.0	3	37.5	19.0
Elymus trachycaulus	3	37.5	4	62.5	1	2.5	2	15.0	3	37.5	31.0
Total Perennial Grasses		75.0		65.0		5.0		30.0		77.5	50.5
Perennial Forbs											
Achillea millefolium			1	2.5					2	15.0	3.5
Total Perennial Forbs		0.0		2.5		0.0		0.0		15.0	3.5
Shrubs and Subshrubs											
Total Shrubs and Subshrubs		0.0		0.0		0.0		0.0		0.0	0.0
Sum of Species Cover		75.0		67.5		5.0		30.0		92.5	54.0
Total Live Vegetation Cover		75.0		67.5		5.0		30.0		92.5	54.0
Litter	2	15.0	2	15.0	4	62.5	2	15.0	2	15.0	24.5
Mulch	0		0		0		1	2.5	1	2.5	1.0
Bare ground	2	15.0	2	15.0	1	2.5	2	15.0	1	2.5	10.0
Total Ground Cover		90.0		82.5		67.5		47.5		110.0	79.5

PLOT 6 - Onsite Treated with Lime and Organic Matter

Table B-6. Vegetation cover at Keating tailings, July 7, 2005.

Life Form and Species	Frame 1 Class	Midpoint Percent	Frame 2 Class	Midpoint Percent	Frame 3 Class	Midpoint Percent	Frame 4 Class	Midpoint Percent	Frame 5 Class	Midpoint Percent	Mean Cover per Plot
Perennial Grasses											
Poa ampla									1	2.5	0.5
Pascopyrum smithii	2	15.0	2	15.0	1	2.5	2	15.0	1	2.5	10.0
Elymus trachycaulus	4	62.5	4	62.5	4	62.5	4	62.5	4	62.5	62.5
Nassella viridula	1	2.5							1	2.5	1.0
Total Perennial Grasses		77.5		80.0		65.0		77.5		70.0	74.0
Perennial Forbs											
Achillea millefolium			1	2.5	2	15.0	2	15.0	1	2.5	7.0
Total Perennial Forbs		0.0		2.5		15.0		15.0		2.5	7.0
Shrubs and Subshrubs											
Total Shrubs and Subshrubs		0.0		0.0		0.0		0.0		0.0	0.0
Sum of Species Cover		77.5		82.5		80.0		92.5		72.5	81.0
Total Live Vegetation Cover		77.5		82.5		80.0		92.5		72.5	81.0
Litter	2	15.0	2	15.0	2	15.0	2	15.0	2	15.0	15.0
Mulch	1	2.5	1	2.5	1	2.5	1	2.5	1	2.5	2.5
Bare ground	0		0		0		0		0		0.0
Total Ground Cover		95.0		100.0		97.5		110.0		90.0	98.5

PLOT 7 - Onsite Control

Table B-7. Vegetation cover at Keating tailings, July 7, 2005.

Life Form and Species	Frame 1 Class	Frame 1 Midpoint Percent	Frame 2 Class	Frame 2 Midpoint Percent	Frame 3 Class	Frame 3 Midpoint Percent	Frame 4 Class	Frame 4 Midpoint Percent	Frame 5 Class	Frame 5 Midpoint Percent	Mean cover per plot
Perennial Grasses											
Poa ampla					1	2.5					0.5
Pascopyrum smithii	1	2.5	1	2.5	1	2.5	1	2.5			2.0
Elymus trachycaulus	1	2.5	1	2.5	1	2.5	1	2.5	1	2.5	2.5
Total Perennial Grasses		5.0		5.0		7.5		5.0		2.5	5.0
Perennial Forbs											
Total Perennial Forbs		0.0		0.0		0.0		0.0		0.0	0.0
Shrubs and Subshrubs											
Total Shrubs and Subshrubs		0.0		0.0		0.0		0.0		0.0	0.0
Sum of Species Cover		5.0		5.0		7.5		5.0		2.5	5.0
Total Live Vegetation Cover		5.0		5.0		7.5		5.0		2.5	5.0
Litter	0	0	0	0	0	0	0	0	0	0	
Mulch	4	62.5	3	37.5	3	37.5	3	37.5	4	62.5	47.5
Bare ground	2	15.0	4	62.5	3	37.5	3	37.5	2	15.0	33.5
Total Ground Cover		67.5		42.5		45.0		42.5		65.0	52.5

PLOT 8 - Onsite Control

Table B-8. Vegetation cover at Keating tailings, July 7, 2005.

Life Form and Species	Frame 1 Class	Frame 1 Midpoint Percent	Frame 2 Class	Frame 2 Midpoint Percent	Frame 3 Class	Frame 3 Midpoint Percent	Frame 4 Class	Frame 4 Midpoint Percent	Frame 5 Class	Frame 5 Midpoint Percent	Mean cover per plot
Perennial Grasses											
Poa ampla	2	15.0	1	2.5	1	2.5	2	15.0			7.0
Pascopyrum smithii	1	2.5	1	2.5	1	2.5	1	2.5	1	2.5	2.5
Elymus trachycaulus	1	2.5	2	15.0	2	15.0	1	2.5			4.0
Total Perennial Grasses		20.0		5.0		20.0		20.0		2.5	13.5
Perennial Forbs											
Total Perennial Forbs		0.0		0.0		0.0		0.0		0.0	0.0
Shrubs and Subshrubs											
Total Shrubs and Subshrubs		0.0		0.0		0.0		0.0		0.0	0.0
Trees											
Populus tremuloides			1	2.5							0.5
Total Trees		0.0		2.5		0.0		0.0		0.0	0.5
Sum of Species Cover		20.0		7.5		20.0		20.0		2.5	14.0
Total Live Vegetation Cover		20.0		7.5		20.0		20.0		2.5	14.0
Litter	0		0		0		0		0		0.0
Mulch	3	37.5	3	37.5	2	15.0	3	37.5	2	15.0	28.5
Bare ground	1	2.5	2	15.0	3	37.5	2	15.0	5	85.0	31.0
Total Ground Cover		57.5		45.0		35.0		57.5		17.5	42.5

Table B-9. Vegetation cover at Keating tailings, July 7, 2005.

PLOT 9 - Onsite Treated with Lime and Organic Matter

Life Form and Species	Frame 1		Frame 2		Frame 3		Frame 4		Frame 5		Mean Cover
	Class	Midpoint Percent	Class	Midpoint Percent	Class	Midpoint Percent	Class	Midpoint Percent	Class	Midpoint Percent	per Plot
Perennial Grasses											
Poa ampla	1	2.5									0.5
Pascopyrum smithii	3	37.5	1	2.5	1	2.5	2	15.0	3	37.5	19.0
Elymus trachycaulus	4	62.5	3	37.5	3	37.5	3	37.5	4	62.5	47.5
Nassella viridula									1	2.5	0.5
Total Perennial Grasses		102.5		40.0		40.0		52.5		102.5	67.5
Perennial Forbs											
Achillea millefolium									1	2.5	0.5
Total Perennial Forbs		0.0		0.0		0.0		0.0		2.5	0.5
Shrubs and Subshrubs											
Total Shrubs and Subshrubs		0.0		0.0		0.0		0.0		0.0	0.0
Sum of Species Cover		102.5		40.0		40.0		52.5		105.0	68.0
Total Live Vegetation Cover		102.5		40.0		40.0		52.5		105.0	68.0
Litter	2	15.0	2	15.0	3	37.5	2	15.0	2	15.0	19.5
Mulch	0	0	3	37.5	2	15.0	1	2.5	1	2.5	11.5
Bare ground	0	0	1	2.5	1	2.5	1	2.5	1	2.5	2.0
Total Ground Cover		117.5		92.5		92.5		70.0		122.5	99.0

PLOT 10 - Onsite Control

Table B-10. Vegetation cover at Keating tailings, July 7, 2005.

Life Form and Species	Frame 1 Class	Midpoint Percent	Frame 2 Class	Midpoint Percent	Frame 3 Class	Midpoint Percent	Frame 4 Class	Midpoint Percent	Frame 5 Class	Midpoint Percent	Mean Cover per Plot
Perennial Grasses											
Pascopyrum smithii	2	15.0	1	2.5			1	2.5		2.5	4.0
Elymus trachycaulus	2	15.0	2	15.0	1	2.5	1	2.5	1	2.5	7.5
Total Perennial Grasses		30.0		17.5		2.5		5.0		2.5	11.5
Perennial Forbs											
Total Perennial Forbs		0.0		0.0		0.0		0.0		0.0	0.0
Shrubs and Subshrubs											
Total Shrubs and Subshrubs		0.0		0.0		0.0		0.0		0.0	0.0
Sum of Species Cover		30.0		17.5		2.5		5.0		2.5	11.5
Total Live Vegetation Cover		30.0		17.5		2.5		5.0		2.5	11.5
Litter	0		0		0		0		0		
Mulch	2	15.0	4	62.5	3	37.5	3	37.5	5	85.0	47.5
Bare ground	2	15.0	1	2.5	4	62.5	2	15.0	1	2.5	19.5
Total Ground Cover		45.0		80.0		40.0		42.5		87.5	59.0

Table B-11. Vegetation cover at Keating tailings, July 7, 2005.

PLOT 11 - Onsite Treated with Lime and Organic Matter

Life Form and Species	Frame 1 Class	Midpoint Percent	Frame 2 Class	Midpoint Percent	Frame 3 Class	Midpoint Percent	Frame 4 Class	Midpoint Percent	Frame 5 Class	Midpoint Percent	Mean Cover per Plot
Perennial Grasses											
Pascopyrum smithii	2	15.0	2	15.0	1	2.5	1	2.5	3	37.5	14.5
Elymus trachycaulus	4	62.5	4	62.5	2	15.0	4	62.5	4	62.5	53.0
Nassella viridula									1	2.5	0.5
Achnatherum hymenoides							1	2.5			0.5
Total Perennial Grasses		77.5		77.5		17.5		67.5		102.5	68.5
Perennial Forbs											
Achillea millefolium					1	2.5	1	2.5			1.0
Total Perennial Forbs		0.0		0.0		2.5		2.5		0.0	1.0
Shrubs and Subshrubs											
Total Shrubs and Subshrubs		0.0		0.0		0.0		0.0		0.0	0.0
Sum of Species Cover		77.5		77.5		20.0		70.0		102.5	69.5
Total Live Vegetation Cover		77.5		77.5		20.0		70.0		102.5	69.5
Litter	2	15.0	2	15.0	2	15.0	2	15.0	2	15.0	15.0
Mulch	1	2.5	1	2.5	4	62.5	2	15.0	1	2.5	17.0
Bare ground	0		0		1	2.5	1	2.5	0		1.0
Total Ground Cover		95.0		95.0		97.5		100.0		120.0	101.5

PLOT 12 - Onsite Control

Table B-12. Vegetation cover at Keating tailings, July 7, 2005.

Life Form and Species	Frame 1 Class	Midpoint Percent	Frame 2 Class	Midpoint Percent	Frame 3 Class	Midpoint Percent	Frame 4 Class	Midpoint Percent	Frame 5 Class	Midpoint Percent	Mean Cover per Plot
Perennial Grasses											
Poa ampla	1	2.5									0.5
Pascopyrum smithii	1	2.5	1	2.5	1	2.5	1	2.5	1	2.5	2.5
Elymus trachycaulus	2	15.0	2	15.0	1	2.5	1	2.5	1	2.5	7.5
Total Perennial Grasses		20.0		17.5		5.0		5.0		5.0	10.5
Annual Grasses											
Hordeum L.					1	2.5					0.5
Total Annual Grasses		0.0		0.0		2.5		0.0		0.0	0.5
Perennial Forbs											
Total Perennial Forbs		0.0		0.0		0.0		0.0		0.0	0.0
Shrubs and Subshrubs											
Total Shrubs and Subshrubs		0.0		0.0		0.0		0.0		0.0	0.0
Sum of Species Cover		20.0		17.5		7.5		5.0		5.0	11.0
Total Live Vegetation Cover		20.0		17.5		7.5		5.0		5.0	11.0
Litter	0		0		0		0		0		
Mulch	3	37.5	2	15.0	5	85.0	3	37.5	5	85.0	52.0
Bare ground	3	37.5	3	37.5	1	2.5	2	15.0	2	15.0	21.5
Total Ground Cover		57.5		32.5		92.5		42.5		90.0	63.0

Appendix C–
Aboveground
Biomass

Table C-1. Aboveground biomass vegetation at Keating tailings, July 7, 2005.
PLOT 1 - Offsite Native Range Site (Frame size is 25 cm x 25 cm)

Species	Frame 1 (g)	Frame 2 (g)	Frame 3 (g)	Frame 4 (g)	Frame 5 (g)		Mean biomass (g/m²) per plot
Achillea millefolium				0.03		0.03	
Pascopyrum smithii	2.34		1.52		2.77	6.63	
Elymus trachycaulus	12.46	34.48	28.06	18.40	40.85	134.25	
Artemisia frigida	1.00					1.00	
Artemisia ludoviciana			0.52			0.52	
Opuntia polyacantha	0.39					0.39	
Poa ampla		0.73			3.66	4.39	
Hesperostipa comata	2.07				0.39	2.46	
Nassella viridula	3.74	2.37		0.77		6.88	
							500.96

Table C-2. Aboveground biomass vegetation at Keating tailings, July 7, 2005.
Plot 2 - Offsite Native Range Site (Frame size is 25 cm x 25 cm)

Species	Frame 1 (g)	Frame 2 (g)	Frame 3 (g)	Frame 4 (g)	Frame 5 (g)		Mean biomass (g/m²) per plot
Achillea millefolium	0.07					0.07	
Achnatherum hymenoides					0.86	0.86	
Pascopyrum smithii	2.66	6.10	3.45	3.36	3.75	19.32	
Elymus trachycaulus	23.09	25.00	24.37	25.40	5.10	102.96	
Artemisia frigida	0.29	0.72			0.76	1.77	
Artemisia ludoviciana	0.43	0.37				0.80	
Poa ampla		0.61			2.38	2.99	
Hesperostipa comata		0.45			7.00	7.45	
Nassella viridula		0.92			2.57	3.49	
							447.07

Table C-3. Aboveground biomass vegetation at Keating tailings, July 7, 2005.
Plot 3 - Offsite Native Range Site (Frame size is 25 cm x 25 cm)

Species	Frame 1 (g)	Frame 2 (g)	Frame 3 (g)	Frame 4 (g)	Frame 5 (g)		Total biomass (g/m²) per plot
Pascopyrum smithii	2.61	5.06	5.05	2.19	2.89	17.80	
Elymus trachycaulus	13.03	31.59	38.39	42.88	7.48	133.37	
Artemisia frigida	0.49				3.48	3.97	
Artemisia ludoviciana					0.82	0.82	
Festuca L.	0.25					0.25	
Nassella viridula		2.23				2.23	
							505.60

Table C-4. Aboveground biomass vegetation at Keating tailings, July 7, 2005.
Plot 4 - Offsite Native Range Site (Frame size is 25 cm x 25 cm)

Species	Frame 1 (g)	Frame 2 (g)	Frame 3 (g)	Frame 4 (g)	Frame 5 (g)		Total biomass (g/m²) per plot
Achillea millefolium		0.12				0.12	
Pascopyrum smithii		3.37	3.76	9.48	1.89	18.50	
Elymus trachycaulus	11.56	27.71	6.72	19.58	36.15	101.72	
Artemisia frigida	0.46	0.84				1.30	
Artemisia ludoviciana		0.12				0.12	
Poa ampla		6.46			1.19	7.65	
Hesperostipa comata	2.36					2.36	
Nassella viridula				2.56	1.28	3.84	
							433.95

Table C-5. Aboveground biomass vegetation at Keating tailings, July 7, 2005.
PLOT 5 - Onsite Treated with Lime and Organic Matter (Frame size is 25 cm x 25 cm)

Species	Frame 1 (g)	Frame 2 (g)	Frame 3 (g)	Frame 4 (g)	Frame 5 (g)		Total biomass (g/m²) per plot
Achillea millefolium				0.20		0.20	
Pascopyrum smithii	10.23	0.76			5.47	16.46	
Elymus trachycaulus	49.27	61.11	12.45	29.17	43.05	195.05	
Hordeum jubatum		1.01				1.01	
Nassella viridula	0.46	0.92			0.43	1.81	
							686.50

Table C-6. Aboveground biomass vegetation at Keating tailings, July 7, 2005.
PLOT 6 - Onsite Treated with Lime and Organic Matter (Frame size is 25 cm x 25 cm)

Species	Frame 1 (g)	Frame 2 (g)	Frame 3 (g)	Frame 4 (g)	Frame 5 (g)		Total biomass (g/m²) per plot
Achillea millefolium				3.25	1.00	4.25	
Pascopyrum smithii	4.49	7.68	3.67	2.05		17.89	
Elymus trachycaulus	55.78	22.59	3.92	28.56	79.49	190.34	
Artemisia ludoviciana					3.14	3.14	
Poa ampla					1.55	1.55	
							694.94

Table C-7. Aboveground biomass vegetation at Keating tailings, July 7, 2005.
PLOT 7 - Onsite Control (Frame size is 25 cm x 25 cm)

Species	Frame 1 (g)	Frame 2 (g)	Frame 3 (g)	Frame 4 (g)	Frame 5 (g)		Total biomass (g/m²) per plot
Pascopyrum smithii	0.94	0.15	1.06	0.64	0.34	3.13	
Elymus trachycaulus		0.71	1.7	1.39		3.80	
							22.18

Table C-8. Aboveground biomass vegetation at Keating tailings, July 7, 2005.
PLOT 8 - Onsite Control (Frame size is 25 cm x 25 cm)

Species	Frame 1 (g)	Frame 2 (g)	Frame 3 (g)	Frame 4 (g)	Frame 5 (g)		Total biomass (g/m²) per plot
Pascopyrum smithii	3.33	2.35	1.00	3.06	0.32	10.06	
Elymus trachycaulus	1.84	5.36	2.08	4.09		13.37	
Poa ampla	3.74	3.18		1.18		8.10	
Populus tremuloides		0.17				0.17	
							101.44

Table C-9. Aboveground biomass vegetation at Keating tailings, July 7, 2005.
PLOT 9 - Onsite Treated with Lime and Organic Matter (Frame size is 25 cm x 25 cm)

Species	Frame 1 (g)	Frame 2 (g)	Frame 3 (g)	Frame 4 (g)	Frame 5 (g)		Total biomass (g/m²) per plot
Pascopyrum smithii		0.45	7.96	1.56	2.92	12.89	
Elymus trachycaulus	76.19	13.51	15.51	21.86	36.70	163.77	
Nassella viridula					3.30	3.30	
							575.81

Table C-10. Aboveground biomass vegetation at Keating tailings, July 7, 2005.
PLOT 10 - Onsite Control (Frame size is 25 cm x 25 cm)

Species	Frame 1 (g)	Frame 2 (g)	Frame 3 (g)	Frame 4 (g)	Frame 5 (g)		Total biomass (g/m²) per plot
Pascopyrum smithii	1.74	1.65	2.13	0.40	0.33	6.25	
Elymus trachycaulus	12.45	2.45		0.60		15.50	
Poa ampla			1.28			1.28	
							73.70

Table C-11. Aboveground biomass vegetation at Keating tailings, July 7, 2005.
PLOT 11 - Onsite Treated with Lime and Organic Matter (Frame size is 25 cm x 25 cm)

Species	Frame 1 (g)	Frame 2 (g)	Frame 3 (g)	Frame 4 (g)	Frame 5 (g)		Total biomass (g/m²) per plot
Achillea millefolium			0.17	1.58		1.75	
Achnatherum hymenoides				2.24		2.24	
Pascopyrum smithii	4.20	2.93	1.55	15.38	6.39	30.45	
Elymus trachycaulus	25.12	42.82	10.55	71.16	42.37	192.02	
Poa ampla				1.19		1.19	
							728.48

Table C-12. Aboveground biomass vegetation at Keating tailings, July 7, 2005.
PLOT 12 - Onsite Control (Frame size is 25 cm x 25 cm)

Species	Frame 1 (g)	Frame 2 (g)	Frame 3 (g)	Frame 4 (g)	Frame 5 (g)		Total biomass (g/m²) per plot
Pascopyrum smithii	0.59	2.41	2.08	0.09	0.60	5.77	
Elymus trachycaulus	0.89	5.18	2.26	2.26	0.54	11.13	
Astragalus spp.					0.03	0.03	
							54.18

Appendix D–Arsenic and Metal Levels in Vegetation

Table D-1. Arsenic and metal levels (mg/kg) in vegetation collected from experimental plots at Keating tailings, July 7, 2005.

		Arsenic	Cadmium	Lead	Copper	Zinc	Mercury
Offsite Control							
VEG1	Western wheatgrass	0.4	<0.05	0.20	3.0	11	<0.1
VEG2	Western wheatgrass	0.3	<0.05	0.11	2.8	11	<0.1
VEG3	Western wheatgrass	<0.3	<0.05	0.06	2.5	12	<0.1
VEG4	Western wheatgrass	<0.3	<0.05	0.07	2.5	11	<0.1
VEG 13	Slender wheatgrass	<0.3	<0.05	<0.11	2.5	9	<0.1
VEG 14	Slender wheatgrass	<0.3	<0.05	0.21	2.6	10	<0.1
VEG 15	Slender wheatgrass	<0.3	<0.05	0.08	2.1	9	<0.1
VEG 16	Slender wheatgrass	<0.3	<0.05	0.06	2.2	7	<0.1
VEG 30	Big bluegrass	0.7	<0.05	0.23	3.4	9	<0.1
VEG 31	Big bluegrass	0.8	0.05	0.14	3.5	9	<0.1
VEG 39	Fringed sagewort	7.8	1.32	9.20	19.0	57	<0.1
Treated Tailings							
VEG5	Western wheatgrass	3.3	0.21	0.47	7.8	34	<0.1
VEG9	Western wheatgrass	0.6	0.80	0.81	11.4	84	<0.1
VEG11	Western wheatgrass	0.3	0.66	0.09	8.1	71	<0.1
VEG 17	Slender wheatgrass	0.9	0.28	0.30	6.1	24	<0.1
VEG 18	Slender wheatgrass	0.7	0.55	0.37	8.8	47	<0.1
VEG 21	Slender wheatgrass	0.8	0.34	0.25	10.1	56	<0.1
VEG 23	Slender wheatgrass	1.3	0.66	0.65	8.9	67	<0.1
VEG 41	Indian ricegrass	0.8	2.13	0.23	10.4	44	<0.1
VEG 40	Cudweed sagewort	2.6	3.62	1.62	27.5	69	<0.1
Untreated Tailings							
VEG7	Western wheatgrass	3.8	5.01	2.75	40.7	319	<0.1
VEG8	Western wheatgrass	1.8	3.30	1.26	16.5	201	<0.1
VEG 12	Western wheatgrass	2.9	1.98	1.86	23.1	129	<0.1
VEG 19	Slender wheatgrass	2.7	4.14	2.00	26.9	289	<0.1
VEG 20	Slender wheatgrass	3.3	3.64	2.33	26.7	240	<0.1
VEG 22	Slender wheatgrass	1.6	2.66	1.16	22.2	176	<0.1
VEG 34	Big bluegrass	2.1	1.87	1.25	20.0	163	<0.1